Oxford First Encyclopedia

My Body

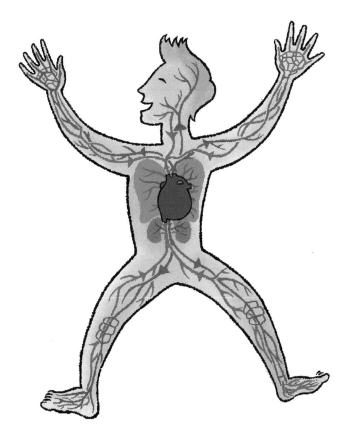

Andrew Langley

OXFORD

OXFORD
UNIVERSITY PRESS

Great Clarendon Street, Oxford OX2 6DP

Oxford University Press is a department of the University of Oxford.
It furthers the University's objective of excellence in research, scholarship,
and education by publishing worldwide in

Oxford New York

Auckland Bangkok Buenos Aires Cape Town Chennai
Dar es Salaam Delhi Hong Kong Istanbul Karachi Kolkata
Kuala Lumpur Madrid Melbourne Mexico City Mumbai Nairobi
São Paulo Shanghai Singapore Taipei Tokyo Toronto

with an associated company in Berlin

Oxford is a registered trade mark of Oxford University Press
in the UK and in certain other countries

© Andrew Langley 1999, 2002

The moral rights of the author have been asserted

Database right Oxford University Press (maker)

First published in 1999
Second edition 2002

British Library Cataloguing in Publication Data available

ISBN 0-19-910970-2

10 9 8 7 6 5 4 3 2

Printed in Malaysia

Contents

My Body

Your body is an amazingly complicated machine, with lots of parts working together. The fuels that keep it going are the food you eat and oxygen from the air. A machine may have hundreds, or even thousands of parts, but your body has millions and millions! Your skin, bones, muscles and all the different organs are made of tiny parts called cells. They all work together so that you can eat, sleep, breathe, run, laugh, cry, shout – and read this book!

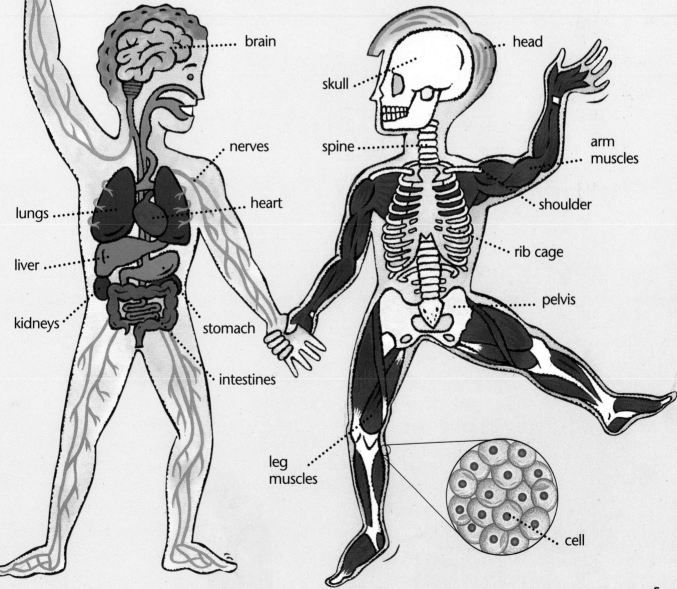

brain

nerves

heart

lungs

liver

kidneys

stomach

intestines

head

skull

spine

arm muscles

shoulder

rib cage

pelvis

leg muscles

cell

Look at me

Look at your face in the mirror. You can see your eyes, your ears, your nose and your mouth. Each of these features is one of your senses. We have five senses altogether – sight, hearing, smell, taste and touch. Without them, we would not know anything about the world around us.

▷ How many different ways of using the senses can you see in this picture?

Sight

You see with your eyes. Each eye has a black dot in the middle, called the pupil. It lets in light, so that you can see what is in front of you. Behind the pupil is a lens. This makes a picture of what you are looking at on the back of the eye.

Touch

You sense touch through your skin. The skin has millions of nerve endings just under the surface. When you touch something, the nerve endings tell you what it feels like. It may be hot, cold, soft, hard, sharp, wet or dry.

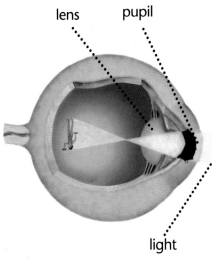

lens   pupil

light

Make a "feely" bag

You use several senses to tell what things are. Try fooling your friends by only letting them use one sense: their sense of touch. Find a plastic bag (one you cannot see through), and put in some grapes with the skins peeled off. Ask your friends to guess what is in the bag by feeling. You could tell them that the grapes are eyeballs, and see what they do!

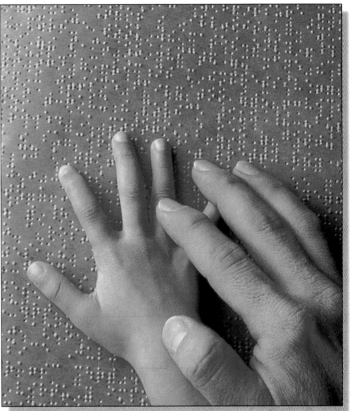

△ You can use one sense to help you with another! Blind people cannot see. But they can read books which have a special kind of "writing" called Braille. Each letter has a code of dots. These dots are printed so that they stick up slightly from the page, and readers can feel them with their fingers.

Sound

You hear with your ears. Sounds are vibrations in the air. The ear flaps on the outside of your head gather sounds from outside, and tiny bones inside your ear make them louder.

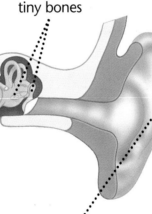

tiny bones

ear flap

Smell and taste

You smell with your nose and taste with your tongue. Smells in the air come in through your nose as you breathe. Your tongue is covered in tiny bumps called taste buds. These tell you whether your food is sweet, salty, bitter or sour. Your sense of smell also helps you to taste things. When you have a cold and cannot smell properly, your food tastes less interesting.

My outside

Your skin covers every bit of you. It protects the inside of your body in three important ways. It helps to keep out germs, it makes you waterproof, and it stops your body from getting too hot or too cold. Your skin is also full of nerve endings. These send messages to the brain about things you touch, telling it how they feel.

Fingerprint fun

Your fingertips have patterns of tiny loops and curves on them. These are your fingerprints. No-one else has fingerprints exactly like yours.
Try painting the tip of your finger and making coloured fingerprints. You could turn them into fingerprint pictures!

Dead on the outside

Did you know that you are dead on the outside? Your skin has two main layers. The outer layer, called the epidermis, is covered in dead cells. But don't worry – there are new cells just underneath. The inner layer is called the dermis. Inside that is a layer of fat, to keep you warm.

Hot and cold

When you get hot, sweat comes out through holes in your skin, called pores. As the sweat dries on your skin, it takes away heat from your body and cools you down. When you get cold, the pores close up so that the sweat stays in. You may start shivering as well. This warms you by making your muscles produce more heat.

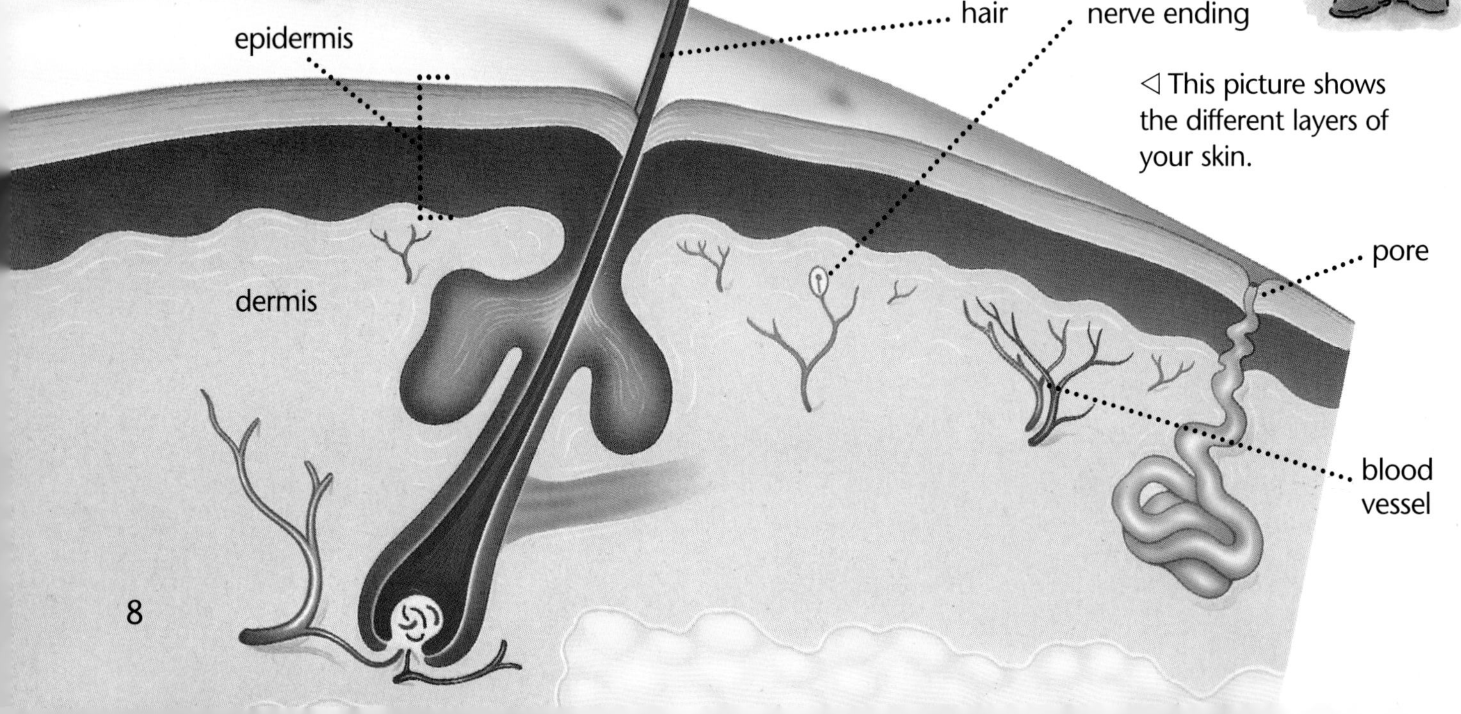

epidermis

dermis

hair   nerve ending

◁ This picture shows the different layers of your skin.

pore

blood vessel

8

Ouch!

You have cut yourself! Your body must work fast, to stop harmful bacteria getting inside you. Your skin and blood work together to do this. First, blood cells clot together to make a patch over the wound, called a scab. Then special white blood cells kill any bacteria that have got in. Under the scab, new skin cells start to grow.

! *Longer and longer*

Your hair is growing all the time (your nails do this too). If you do not cut your hair, it will normally grow to about a metre in length, then stop. But some people's hair does not stop growing. The longest hair in the world is nearly 4 metres long!

Skin colour

What colour is your skin? People's skin can be many different colours, from dark brown to pale pink. It all depends how much melanin (dark colouring) you have in your skin.

▷ Pale-skinned people have less melanin in their skin. This lets more sunlight into the skin. The sunlight warms the body, which is good when the weather is cold. But it also means that the skin burns more easily.

△ Dark-skinned people have a lot of melanin in their skin. This helps to block out the sun's rays and protect the skin from sunburn.

Bones and muscles

There is a skeleton inside you. A skeleton is a framework of bones joined together. It holds up your body and gives it shape. There are more than 200 bones in your body, with more than 600 muscles fixed to them! Together the muscles and bones work to move you about.

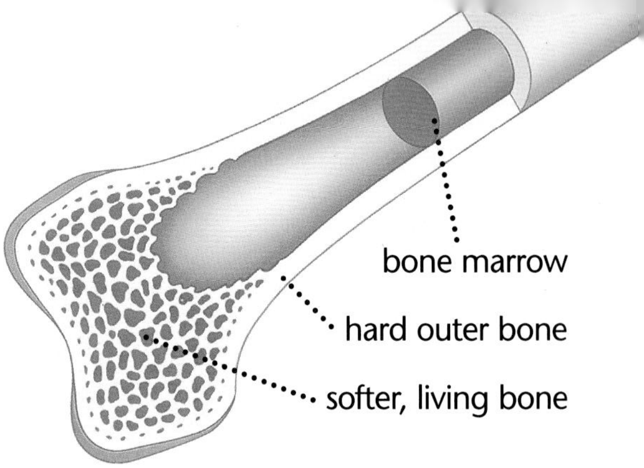

bone marrow

hard outer bone

softer, living bone

△ Bones are hard on the outside, but inside them are softer, living cells. Some big bones, like this thigh bone, have a tube in the middle. The tube is filled with bone marrow, a soft tissue which makes new cells for your blood.

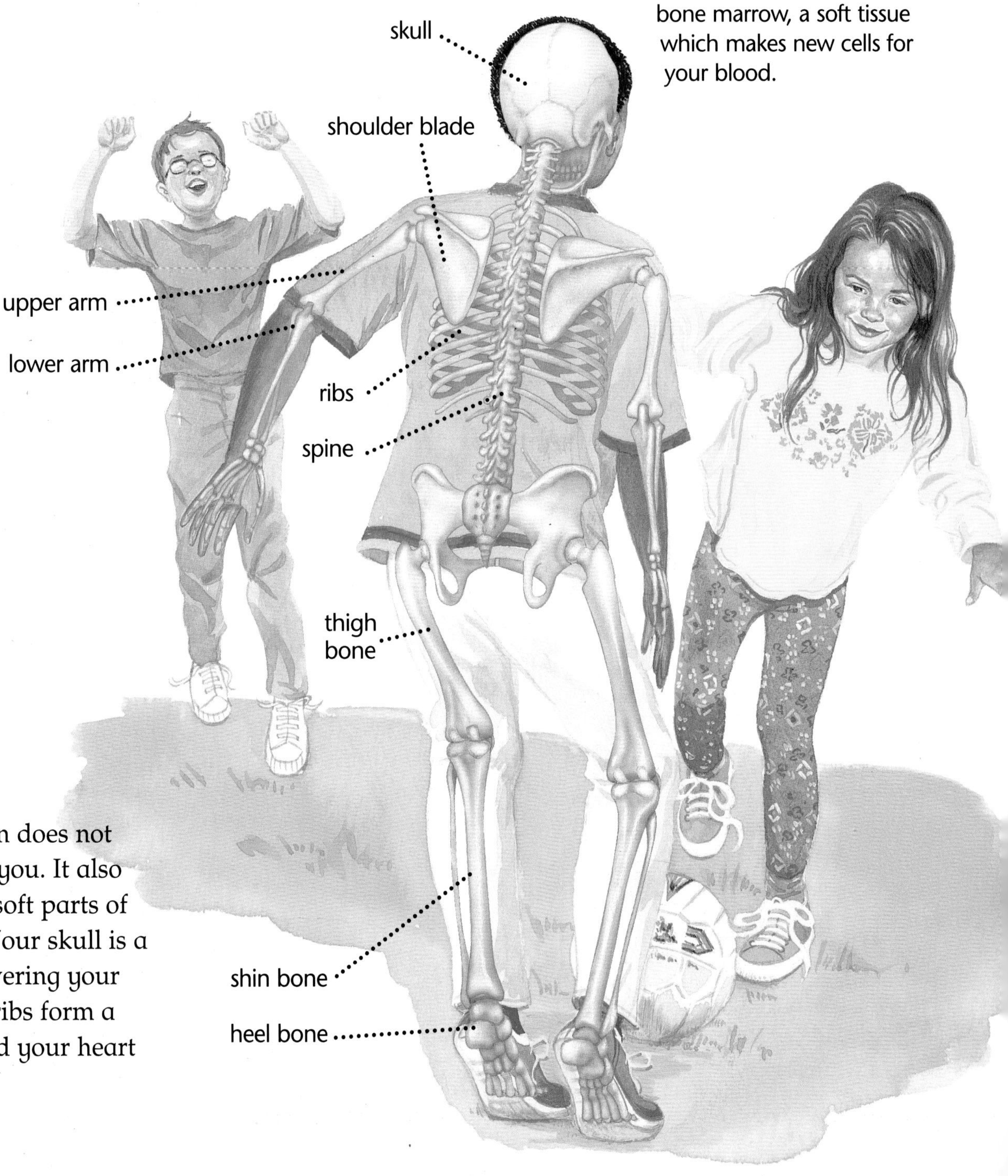

skull

shoulder blade

upper arm

lower arm

ribs

spine

thigh bone

Bones

Your skeleton does not just support you. It also protects the soft parts of your body. Your skull is a hard box covering your brain. Your ribs form a cage to guard your heart and lungs.

shin bone

heel bone

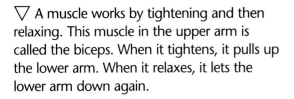
▽ A muscle works by tightening and then relaxing. This muscle in the upper arm is called the biceps. When it tightens, it pulls up the lower arm. When it relaxes, it lets the lower arm down again.

biceps tightens ⋯

biceps ⋯ relaxes

▷ Each muscle is a bundle of thousands of muscle fibres.

Joints

Joints are the places where your bones meet and join. The bones are held together by strong cords called ligaments. Some joints can move in any direction. Your shoulder and hip joints are like this. Other joints, like the elbows and knees, can only bend in one direction.

Muscles

A muscle can only do one thing – pull. But all the muscles in your body use their pulling power to do a huge number of jobs. Some only work when you tell them to. These muscles move your body, making it walk or run. Others, such as the muscles that make you breathe, work all the time, even when you are asleep. The most important muscle of all is your heart, which pumps blood around your body.

◁ By using our muscles and bones together, we can make our bodies move in all sorts of amazing ways.

! **Busy muscles!**

The muscles that move your eyes are the busiest in the body. They tighten or relax more than 100,000 times every day!

Lungs and breathing

In…out…in…out. All day and night, we have to go on breathing. When we breathe in, our lungs fill up with air. This contains the oxygen we need to keep us alive. The oxygen goes into our blood. When we breathe out, we push the air out again. Now it contains carbon dioxide, which we want to get rid of.

Filling the lungs

You have two lungs. Around them, your ribs form a protective cage. Below the lungs is a muscle called the diaphragm.

Endless blood vessels

If all the tiny blood vessels in your lungs were laid out in one straight line, they would stretch for nearly 2,400 kilometres! That's all the way from London to Athens, in Greece!

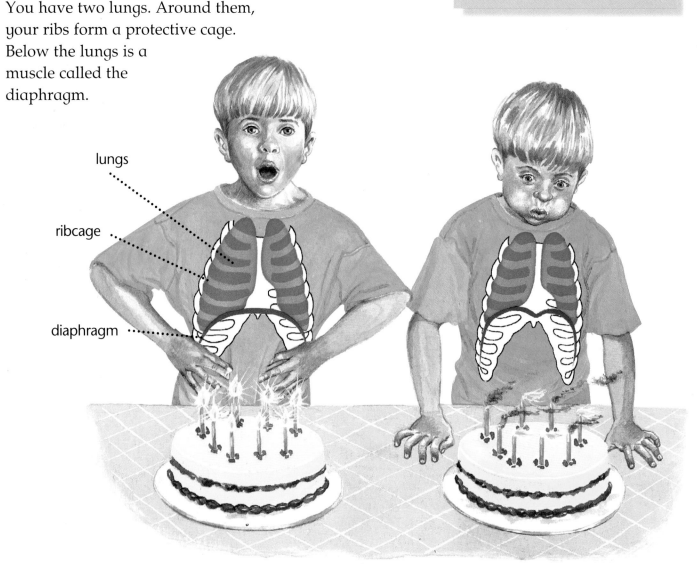

lungs

ribcage

diaphragm

△ When you breathe in, the diaphragm tightens. At the same time, other muscles pull your ribs outwards. This makes your chest and lungs expand, sucking in air through your mouth.

△ To breathe out, the diaphragm and rib muscles relax. Your chest gets smaller again. Your lungs are squashed, and the air in them is squeezed out.

12

Inside your lungs

Your lungs are full of tiny air tubes. At the ends of these tubes are little air bags, surrounded by very thin blood vessels. The oxygen from the air passes through the bags and into the blood vessels. At the same time, carbon dioxide passes from the blood vessels into the lungs.

air tube ....

air bags ....

.... blood vessels

△ Some people suffer from an illness called asthma. A muscle tightens in the tubes leading into the lungs. This makes the tubes narrower, and it is hard for the person to breathe. A puff from a special inhaler can make the muscle relax again.

Breathing fast and slow

When you are asleep, you breathe slowly and gently. Your body is still, so it only needs a small amount of oxygen. When you run about, your body needs more oxygen so you breathe more quickly. Even after you stop running, your body needs to catch up on its oxygen supplies, so you keep panting. Phew!

Test your lungs

Find out how much breath you have in your lungs. Fill a bottle with water, and stand it upside down in a bowl of water (make sure the bottle is full). Put one end of a plastic tube, or a bendy drinking straw, into the bottle. Now take one deep breath and blow (gently!) through the tube. Try and empty your lungs. All the air from your lungs will now be trapped in the bottle.

Pumping the blood

Blood is your body's transport system.
The cells in your body need oxygen to stay alive, and food so that they can grow.
Blood carries oxygen and food to all your cells. It also carries carbon dioxide and other waste materials away from the cells, so that your body can get rid of them. Blood is always on the move. Your heart pumps it through a network of tubes called blood vessels.
These reach every single part of you.

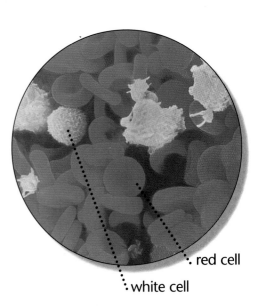

red cell

white cell

△ Blood is made of cells, which float in a watery liquid called plasma. The red cells carry the oxygen (and give blood its red colour). The white cells help to defend your body against germs.

Beating time !

Your heart beats about 70 times a minute. But an elephant's heart only beats 25 times a minute. A robin's heart beats 1000 times a minute!

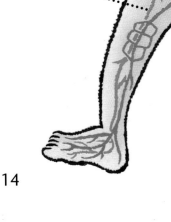

heart ....

lungs

artery ....

vein ....

Circulation

Blood flows around your body all the time. Your heart is the pump that makes it move. It takes about one minute for blood to travel from your heart to your feet and back again. This is called the circulation of the blood. There are two main kinds of blood vessel – arteries and veins. Arteries carry blood filled with oxygen. Veins carry blood filled with carbon dioxide and other waste materials.

Heartbeats

Your heart is a muscle about as big as your fist.
Inside, there are four main parts, or chambers.
Each one is a separate pump. The heart muscle
tightens and relaxes about 70 times every minute.
At each "beat" it pushes blood through
the heart, and out to the
lungs and the body.

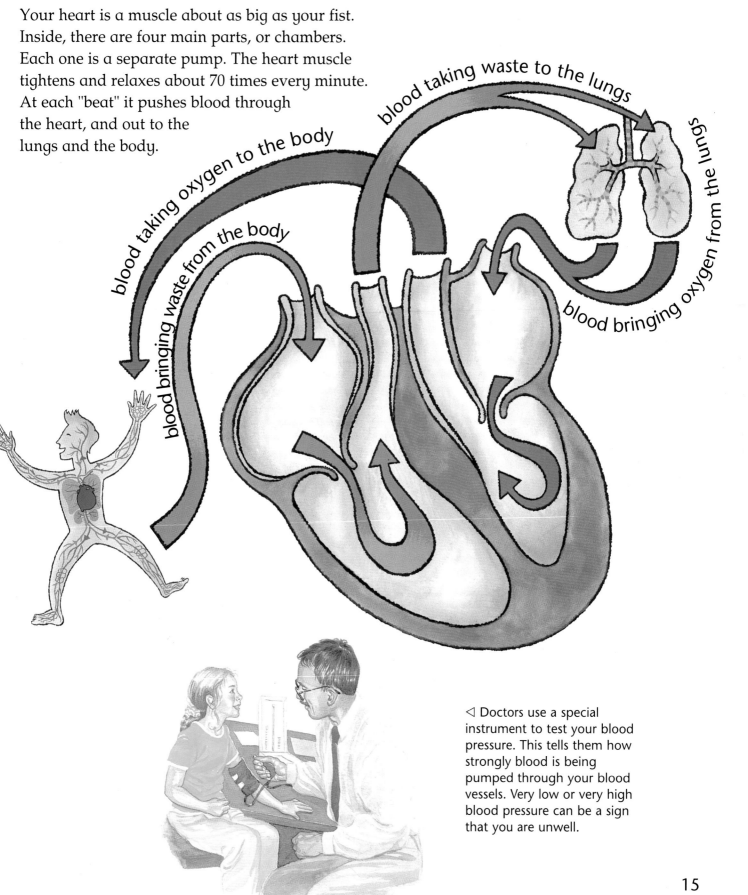

blood taking waste to the lungs

blood taking oxygen to the body

blood bringing oxygen from the lungs

blood bringing waste from the body

◁ Doctors use a special
instrument to test your blood
pressure. This tells them how
strongly blood is being
pumped through your blood
vessels. Very low or very high
blood pressure can be a sign
that you are unwell.

15

My brain and nerves

Inside your head is your brain. This is the control centre of your body. Your brain does your thinking and remembering, and sends out orders to the body about speaking, moving and feeling. It is connected to the rest of your body by cords called nerves. The nerves carry messages between the brain and the body.

▷ Your brain looks grey and wrinkled, like a giant walnut. It has several different parts, each with its own job to do. Each of your five senses has its own area of the brain.

A bundle of nerves

Messages from your brain go into your spinal cord. This is a bundle of nerves running down the middle of your back. Smaller nerves branch off from the spinal cord to every part of your body. The whole network is called your nervous system.

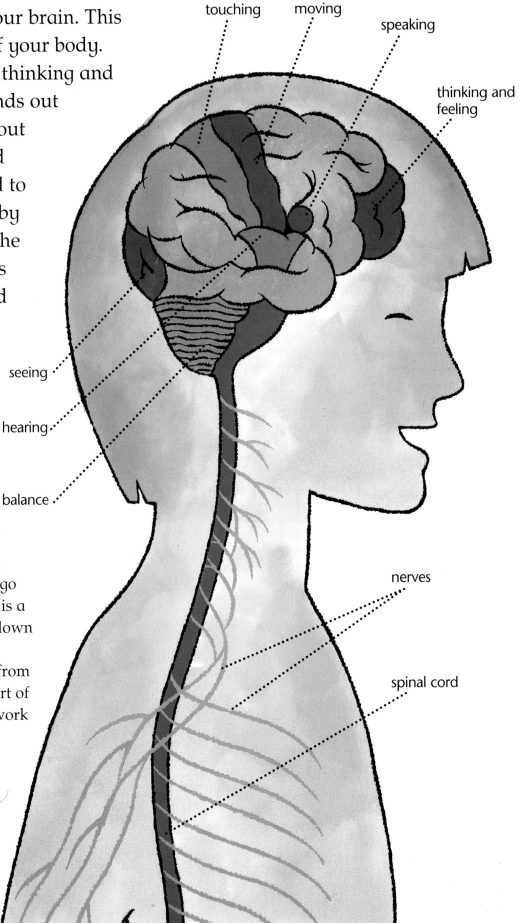

touching

moving

speaking

thinking and feeling

seeing

hearing

balance

nerves

spinal cord

16

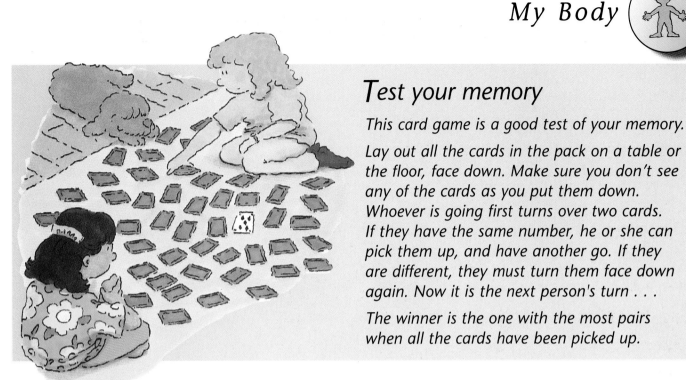

Test your memory

This card game is a good test of your memory.

Lay out all the cards in the pack on a table or the floor, face down. Make sure you don't see any of the cards as you put them down. Whoever is going first turns over two cards. If they have the same number, he or she can pick them up, and have another go. If they are different, they must turn them face down again. Now it is the next person's turn . . .

The winner is the one with the most pairs when all the cards have been picked up.

The brain in action

Your brain is always busy, getting messages then sending its own messages out. Here's how the brain goes into action when you meet someone you know.

1. You see someone walking towards you. Your eyes send a picture of the person to your brain.

2. Your brain recognizes the picture. It is your friend Alfie! You want to say hello. Your brain sends a message to your arm, and another to your mouth.

3. Your arm obeys the order, and starts to wave. Your mouth shouts out "Hello, Alfie!".

! Quick thinking

Messages whizz to and from the brain at speeds of up to 290 kilometres per hour. That's faster than the fastest express train!

What happens to food?

Like a car, your body needs fuel to keep it going. A car runs on petrol: you keep going with food. The food gives you energy and helps you to grow. But first your body has to break down the food into its different parts. Some parts are useful to the body, others are waste. This process is called digestion.

A tube through your body

Food travels through your body along a long tube called the gut. The journey may take over a day. Your gut is coiled up inside your body, and is more than six metres long. It is made up of several different parts, each with its own job to do.

Food goes into your body through the mouth. Your teeth break it up, then your tongue pushes it to the back of your mouth. Gulp!

Muscles in your gullet squeeze the food straight down into the stomach.

The stomach muscles churn up the food with special liquids, which help to break the food down.

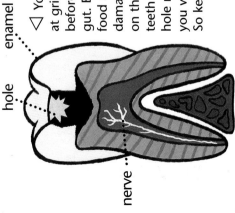

▽ Your teeth are good at grinding up your food before it goes to your gut. But sugar and other food and drink can damage the hard enamel on the outside. Your teeth can get holes. If a hole reaches the nerve, you will get toothache. So keep your teeth clean!

hole   enamel

nerve

rectum

In the small intestine, all the useful parts of the food are absorbed into your body. They pass through the intestine wall and into your blood.

The parts of the food that are left in the gut are waste. This waste goes on into the large intestine and leaves the body through the rectum.

Liver and kidneys

Your liver is one of the busiest parts of your body. It has nearly 500 different jobs to do! Blood comes to the liver from your intestines, carrying useful materials from your food. The liver takes the goodness out of the food and sends it on for other parts of the body to use.

Your kidneys help to keep your blood clean. As blood passes through them, they take out unwanted material and turn it into a liquid called urine. Urine is wee. It is stored in your bladder until you go to the toilet.

liver

kidney

bladder

! A food mountain

During your lifetime, you will eat about 50 tonnes of food, and drink about 50,000 litres of liquid.

19

Being born

This is the story of how a baby grows. It takes two people to make a baby – a mother and a father. Inside the mother is an egg, smaller than a full stop. Inside the father are lots of sperms, even tinier than the egg. The story begins when the sperms travel from the father's body into the mother's body.

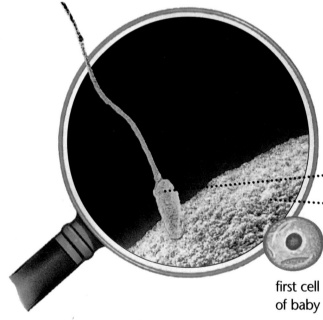

◁ This picture has been magnified many times. It shows a sperm joining up with an egg. The sperm looks a bit like a tadpole.

..... sperm

.... egg

first cell of baby

umbilical cord

this is the baby's real size ....

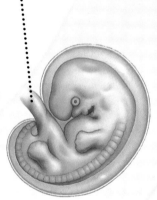

The baby begins

The sperms travel through the mother's body until they reach the egg. Then one sperm joins with the egg, and together they make the first cell of the new baby. The baby starts to grow in a part of the mother's body called the "uterus". The egg splits to make two cells . . . then four . . . then eight, and so on.

uterus ....

△ This baby is about six weeks old. It is no longer just a ball of cells, but it is very small. The baby gets food from its mother, through a special tube called the umbilical cord.

▽ After just three months, the baby is fully formed. It has arms and legs, fingers and toes, as well as eyes, ears, nose and a mouth. But it is still very tiny. (The purple shape shows the baby's real size.)

▽ After seven months the baby has grown much bigger (the purple shape shows its real size). Babies in the uterus sleep and wake, just like us. Some scientists even think that they have dreams. The baby grows for two more months, until it is nine months old. Then it is born.

▷ This baby has just been born. The muscles in the mother's uterus have pushed the baby out into the world. It does not need its umbilical cord any more, so the doctor cuts it. The newborn baby feeds on milk from its mother's breasts.

Growing up

From the moment you are born, you grow very quickly. You go on growing all through childhood. But it is not just your body that changes. You find out about the world around you, and about how to do things. You learn how to get on with other people. You go on changing all through your life, learning new skills and having new experiences.

! *Shrinking every day*

Every day, you shrink by about 8 millimetres! As you stand or sit, your weight pushes down on your spine and makes you shorter. But at night, when you lie down, your spine relaxes and stretches out again.

◁ Babies learn quickly. Soon they can smile and laugh, grip with their hands, roll over and make all sorts of noises. By the age of two, they can walk and talk.

▷ By the age of eight, children can use their bodies to run, dance and play games. Their world has become much bigger. They go to school, and have friends to share jokes and secrets.

△ From about ten, boys and girls slowly begin to turn into adults. Girls become more rounded, and their breasts start to grow. Boys grow more hair on their bodies, and their voices get deeper. Soon, boys and girls become interested in going out together.

▽ By about twenty, children have changed into adults. Their bodies are fully developed, and they stop growing taller. Now they are ready to have babies of their own.

△ As people get older, their bodies often slow down. Many people stop working and have more leisure time. Their own children have grown up, but they may have grandchildren, or even great-grandchildren who come to visit them.

Living longer

Today we grow more food and have better medicines than in the past, so people live longer. A hundred years ago, people in the USA lived on average to the age of 47. Today, someone living in the USA can expect to live to 75 or more.

Illness

You feel hot. You shiver. Your head aches. What is happening? You are ill! Your body is under attack from tiny germs. There are many sorts of germs, and they cause many different illnesses. Some, such as chickenpox or a cold, are not very serious. But others can be dangerous.

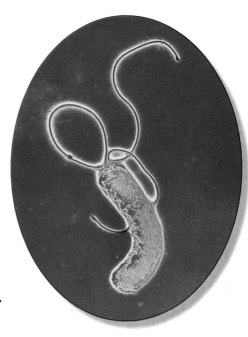

◁ The germ in this picture is called a bacterium. It has been magnified many times.

Getting ill

You can catch an illness from someone else if germs from them get into your body. Germs carry some diseases from one person to another. These are called infectious diseases. The germs travel through the air, or live in food, or get passed on when people cough or sneeze.

▷ Your body can fight off some illnesses by itself. The best way to cure a bad cold or flu is to stay at home and rest in bed.

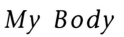

At the doctor's

Sometimes when you are ill, you need to go to see the doctor. Doctors often listen to your chest with a special instrument called a stethoscope. They may also give you medicines or pills, to help fight off germs.

Hospitals

If you are very ill you will have to go to hospital. You may have a serious disease, or have had a bad accident. At the hospital, doctors and nurses give you special care. If something has gone wrong inside your body, you may need an operation. You are taken to a special room called an operating theatre, where you are put to sleep for a short time. Then the doctor can operate on you.

△ All through history, scientists have invented new medicines, new machines and new ways to fight against disease. One important invention is the X-ray machine, which can take pictures of the insides of our bodies. This photograph shows an early X-ray machine.

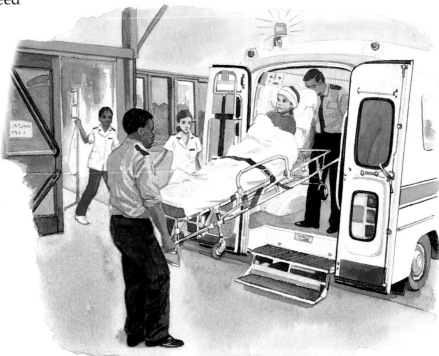

▷ If someone has an accident, an ambulance will come to take them to the hospital. The ambulance workers are trained to help people who have been badly hurt.

A healthy life

You can fight against many kinds of illness – before they even start! Disease has less of a chance if you keep your body fit and healthy. Here are three important ways to do that:

Keep clean

Keeping your body clean helps get rid of germs. If these germs got into your body, they could make you ill. Always wash your hands after using the toilet, and before you touch any food.

Keep moving

Your body likes to be given work to do. Walking, running, swimming and cycling are all good kinds of exercise. Exercise keeps your heart and other muscles in shape, and your bones strong. It gets your blood flowing quickly through your body. All these things make your body healthier.

Eat well

Everyone knows that too many fatty or sugary foods are bad for you. But it is not good to eat too much of any one kind of food. Make sure that your meals contain a mixture of good things: carbohydrate foods such as bread and pasta, fatty foods such as milk and cheese, and high-protein foods such as meat and fish.

△ This food pyramid is a guide to healthy eating. At the bottom are the foods you should eat most of. Only eat a little of the foods right at the top.

Glossary

Glossary

artery a tube or vessel that carries blood away from the heart.

bacteria very simple creatures made of a single cell. Some bacteria cause disease.

biceps a large muscle in the arm, which flexes the elbow.

bone marrow soft tissue inside your bones, where new blood cells are made.

carbon dioxide a gas in the air. When we breathe out, we get rid of unwanted carbon dioxide from our bodies.

cells tiny parts from which all living things are made.

chickenpox an illness where you have itchy spots on the skin and a high temperature.

dermis the living part of the skin, which is below the outer level, or epidermis.

diaphragm a large muscle below the lungs, between the chest and the lower body. It helps with breathing.

digestion the process which breaks down food in our stomachs, so that it can be used in the body.

epidermis the outer layer of the skin.

fibres thin strands or threads. Muscles are made of fibres.

fuel something which is used up to produce energy, for example by burning it.

germ a tiny living creature, which can cause disease.

gullet the throat.

intestine part of the digestive system that connects to the stomach.

kidneys the organs which help to take waste materials out of the blood.

ligament a band of fibres connecting bones or muscles.

liver the organ in the body which helps to make blood and process food.

melanin a dark colouring found in the skin.

muscle a bundle of fibres that tightens or relaxes to move part of the body.

nerves thin fibres that carry electrical messages to and from the brain.

oxygen a gas in the air, which we need to breathe to stay alive.

pores tiny holes in the skin of an animal, which let out sweat and help to keep it cool.

spinal cord the bundle of nerves that is protected by the bones of the spine.

staple food the most important food grown or eaten in a region.

stethoscope an instrument for listening to sounds inside the body.

urine liquid carrying waste material from the body.

uterus the place inside the body of female mammals where babies develop.

vein a tube or vessel that carries blood to the heart.

Index

Index

P

pelvis   5
plasma   14

R

rectum   19
ribs   5, 10, 12

S

senses   6–7, 16
shins   10
shoulders   10
sight   6, 16, 17
skeleton   5, 10
skin   5, 8–9
skull   5, 10

smell   6–7
sneezing   24
sound   7
sperm   20
spinal cord   16
spine   5, 10, 22
stomach   5, 18
sunburn   9
sweat   8

T

talking   16, 22
taste   6–7
teeth   18
thighs   10
thinking   16
tongue   18
touch   6, 7, 8, 16

U

urine   19
uterus   20–21

V

veins   14

W

walking   22, 26
washing   26

X

X-ray   25

Acknowledgements

Abbreviations: t = top; b = bottom; c = centre; l = left; r = right; (back) = background; (fore) = foreground.

Illustrations
Cover Tony Kerrins/Steve Weston; cover tr Michael Courtney; back cover tl Michael Courtney; back cover b Steve Weston; 3 Clive Goodyer; 4 Scot Ritchie; 5 Clive Goodyer; 6–7, 7t Scot Ritchie; 6b, 7c Michael Courtney; 8t Julie Park; 8c Scot Ritchie; 8b Michael Courtney; 9tl Lynne Willey; 9tr Scot Ritchie; 10t Michael Courtney; 10b (back) Lynne Willey; 10b (fore) Steve Weston; 11t Clive Goodyer; 12 (back) Lynne Willey; 12 (fore) Steve Weston; 13tl Steve Weston/Clive Goodyer; 13bl, bc Lynne Willey; 13br Scot Ritchie; 14b, 15t Clive Goodyer; 15b Lynne Willey; 16 Clive Goodyer; 17tl, br, bc, bl Scot Ritchie; 17c Clive Goodyer; 18–19 Clive Goodyer; 20tr Scot Ritchie; 20cr, 21 Michael Courtney; 22, 23b, 23tr Scot Ritchie; 23tl Lynne Willey; 24 b Lynne Willey; 25tl Scot Ritchie; 25b Lynne Willey; 26t Lynne Willey; 26c Clive Goodyer; 26b Scot Ritchie.

Photographs
The publishers would like to thank the following for permission to reproduce photographs:
7tr Image Bank; 9bl, br Oxford University Press; 11b, 13 tr, 14t, 20cl Science Photo Library; 21br Robert Harding; 24t, 25tr Science Photo Library.